LIVING GENEROUSLY
GIVING GENEROUSLY

Spiritual Discipline of Stewardship

by Bob Crossman

© 2020 Robert O. Crossman

Living Generously / Giving Generously: The Spiritual Discipline of Stewardship

Photo Credit: The cover photo and all but a dozen of the photographs in this book came from www.Pixabay.com where it states on their website: *"You can copy, modify, distribute, and use the images, even for commercial purposes, all without asking for permission or giving credits to the artist."*

ISBN 978-0-9996578-1-2 $14.99

Living Generously / Giving Generously: The Spiritual Discipline of Stewardship

Bob Crossman is the Author of

Living Generously / Giving Generously: Spiritual Discipline of Stewardship

Preach Grace: 480 Sermons From a New Church in Conway, Arkansas;

The New Church Handbook: Nuts and Bolts of Planting New Churches;

Committed to Christ: Six Steps to a Generous Life; and

Living Your Commitment to Christ.

**He has three resources available free on the internet.
(Just google the titles below to locate them.)**
50 Ways to Increase Worship Attendance;
50 Ways to Welcome a New Pastor or Associate Pastor; and
50 Ways to Take Church to the Community.

Bob has over forty years of experience in the ministry, serving as pastor or staff member in churches ranging in size from 13 to 3,000, and as an Annual Conference and General Agency staff member. From 2012 to 2018, Bob was deployed to the South Central Jurisdiction as a New Church Strategist for Path 1 at Discipleship Ministries.

As pastor of a new church in Conway, Arkansas, the church grew from the initial group of 48 growing to over 500 in worship and 1,000 in the church family, witnessing 200 baptisms, receiving 270 professions and reaffirmations of faith, and membership transfers from 23 different denominations.

Bob is a recipient of the Denman Evangelism Award and has received Doctor of Ministry and Masters of Theology degrees from Perkins School of Theology, SMU in evangelism and Methodist History. He also received a Bachelors degree from Hendrix College. He has been a certified Minister of Evangelism since 1984.

Bob and Marcia have been married for 47 years and make their home in Conway, Arkansas near their two sons and five grandchildren. His wife Marcia, an Elder in the Arkansas Conference, recently retired after 16 years as Archivist in the United Methodist Collection at Hendrix College's Bailey Library in Conway, Arkansas.

Table of Contents

Chapter One
What Does The Lord Expect From Disciples? . 9

Chapter Two
How to Implant High Expectation Stewardship DNA Into Your Church 33

Chapter Three
Create a Stewardship Ripple Effect in your Church 55

Chapter Four
48 Ways to Improve Your Annual Stewardship Campaign 95

FOREWORD

It's not just giving generously – it's living generously. That is the theme of this book, and I believe it's the invitation we receive from the Lord in the New Testament.

I am proposing a holistic discipleship education emphasis which places financial giving within the context of what the Lord expects of those who seek to be faithful disciples of the Lord. The six steps are not steps toward earning one's salvation, but rather six steps toward a generous life in response to salvation already received from Christ.

It is NOT simply an annual financial campaign for the local church.

The focus is not on the church's needs, but rather upon each individual's need to respond generously to the saving Grace of Jesus Christ - with their hearts and with their hands

It is my prayer that this book will help you to lead your congregation to become deeply devoted disciples of Jesus.

The basic content of this book was first prepared for the Stewardship Summit of the South Carolina Conference of the United Methodist Church. I appreciate their invitation to lead their biennial stewardship summit.

In preparation for that summit, I required the participants to read Clif Christopher's book, *God vs Money*. In recognition of that, in the last chapter I refer to that source and quote Clif Christopher about a dozen times. Clif's book, *God vs Money*, is an excellent resource, and I encourage you to purchase it at Cokesbury.com or Amazon.com.

CHAPTER ONE

I want to begin by grounding my remarks on several verses of scripture that speak directly to the topic before us.

> In this way we remember
> the Lord Jesus' words:
> *"It is more blessed to give than to receive."*
> Acts 20:35b (CEB)

> Everyone should give whatever they have
> decided in their heart.
> They shouldn't give with hesitation
> or because of pressure.
> God loves a cheerful giver.
> 2 Corinthians 9: 7 (CEB)

Your way of life should be free from the love of
money, and you should be content with what you have.
After all, he has said,
"I will never leave you or abandon you."
This is why we can confidently say,
The Lord is my helper, and I won't be afraid.
What can people do to me?
Hebrews 13:5-6 (CEB)

---

†

Jesus said, *"No household servant can serve two
masters. Either you will hate the one and love the
other, or you will be loyal to the one and have
contempt for the other.
You cannot serve God and wealth."*
The Pharisees, who were money-lovers,
heard all this and sneered at Jesus.
Luke 16: 13-14 (CEB)

---

†

Concerning the collection of money for God's people:
you should do what I have directed the churches in
Galatia to do. On the first day of the week, each of you
should set aside whatever you can afford from what
you earn so that the collection won't be delayed until I
come. Then when I get there, I'll send whomever you
approve to Jerusalem with
letters of recommendation to bring your gift.
I Corinthians 16: 1-3 (CEB)

Living Generously / Giving Generously: The Spiritual Discipline of Stewardship

†

Looking up, Jesus saw rich people throwing their gifts into the collection box for the temple treasury. He also saw a poor widow throw in two small copper coins worth a penny. He said, *"I assure you that this poor widow has put in more than them all. All of them are giving out of their spare change. But she from her hopeless poverty has given everything she had to live on."*
Luke 21: 1-4 (CEB)

---

†††

Powerful scriptures. Biblical texts worthy of building one's life upon. Are these Biblical quotes an accurate description of your lifestyle? If Jesus were to examine how you have lived this past week at work, play, school and at home... if Jesus were to look at the checks you've written this month, the funds you've transferred, and your credit card statements... would Jesus say to you, *"Well done, my good and faithful servant"*?
I wonder?

I wonder what Jesus says when he examines my life choices?

I wonder?

†††

40th Wedding Anniversary

I visited Elizabeth and Ansel in the hospital. They had been married some 45 years or so. They did not tell me they were in love - it showed. Elizabeth was in St. Vincent Hospital and had been for weeks. Ansel never left her side. He attempted to sleep in the little chair provided by the hospital. He jumped up in the middle of the night when Elizabeth felt nauseous. He jumped up in the early hours when her incision hurt. He jumped up when the food tray arrived, and he fed her, coaxing her to try a bite. He got her cool towels for her forehead. Ansel fetched a basin when Elizabeth was nauseous, and held her close. This went on for weeks and weeks and weeks. He had cancer too – prostate cancer, skin cancer and brain cancer – but you would never know it. He hurt every time he lay down, but he never said a word of complaint. He needed to see his own doctor, but he would not leave the side of his wife. Ansel needed to be in a hospital bed just as much as Elizabeth – but you see, he loved her. You see, in the end, love comes down to this.

The hospital staff said, *"Ansel, go home with your daughter. I promise we will take care of her."* He answered, *"No, Lizbeth needs me. I'm okay. I'll take care of her. This chair makes a pretty good bed. They bring me food to eat and I can shower here."*

"Ansel, you can't keep this up. You have to go home and rest." Answer, *"I keep my promises."* Promises? What promises? *"When Elizabeth and I married forty years ago, I took a vow at the altar to be faithful to her for better and for worse, for richer and for poorer, in sickness and in health. All these years I have tried to be faithful to that vow."*

And he added, *"I never thought about doing anything else because I love her."*

✝✝✝

Keeping that sacred vow is not a Hollywood scene with Burt Reynolds and Sally Fields, Tom Cruise and Kelly McGillis, or Ross and Rachel. Rather, keeping that vow of love comes down to, *"Would you get me a glass of water."*

You see, in the end, love is not a smoldering glance across the dance floor, not the clink of crystal campaign glasses, not a picnic spread on a field of summer clover, or sitting on the deck of a cruise ship holding hands at sunset.

But love comes down to, *"Hold my hand, I'm scared... I'm sick... I'm lonely."*

The wedding vows put it this way: *"In the name of God, I, take you, as my spouse, to have and to hold from this day forward, for better, for worse, for richer, for poorer, in sickness and in health, to love and to cherish, until we are parted by death. This is my solemn vow."*

†††

Isn't that great? Isn't that wonderful? Just a simple human life lived with absolute honor – absolute integrity.

And yet, it is that kind of life that God blesses. Not the flashy life, not the sensational life, and not the life that

is full of glitter and sparkle. God blesses the simple life that's lived honestly – the simple life that's lived with great honor and integrity.

Do you suppose?

Do you suppose you could faithfully follow the wisdom in the Bible verses above?

Living Generously / Giving Generously: The Spiritual Discipline of Stewardship

Do you suppose you could keep your promises?

Do you suppose you could live your life with such integrity?

Do you suppose God might be able to put that kind of trust in you?

Once upon a time, everyone of us stood before our local congregation and made a vow, a promise to our local church and to the Lord. That promise included being faithful in our participation in the church, our prayer life, our presence in worship, our financial gifts, our service, and in sharing the Good News of Jesus Christ with others.

• How's that working for you?

• Are you keeping your vows?

• Tell me about your prayer life.

• Tell me about your worship attendance frequency.

• Tell me about your financial support of the church. Tell me, how many years have you given 10% of your income through the church?

• Tell me about the variety of ways you give your time to serve through the church.

• Tell me about the last time you shared the faith and invited a neighbor, friend or co-worker to join you at your church in the journey toward discipleship.

• Tell me about another time.

• Tell me about another time.

• Are you a person with integrity?

†††

What is integrity? It seems to have something to do with a harmony between what we believe and what we actually do. A harmony between the beliefs of our faith and activity of our hands. A harmony between God's moral principles and our life-styles.

• Maybe you and I need to become persons of integrity, too, before it's too late.

- Maybe we've not been faithful in our prayers, presence, gifts, service and witness in the past.

- Maybe we've botched it - in lots and lots of ways.

- But listen to this: by God, what's in the past is in the past.

- By God, we can **become** a person of integrity.

- By God, there is no reason we can not begin that transformation today!

(Perhaps this is a good place to stop reading and pray. Ask the Lord for forgiveness and ask for God to send the Holy Spirit to strengthen you for a journey toward Holy and Generous Living.)

†††

That's what I want to talk about: making a commitment to offer nothing less than our personal best. Making a commitment to be the very best disciple we can possibly be, and discovering ways we might invite our congregation to join us in that journey.

†††

In the Biblical passage I shared above from the 21st chapter of Luke, *{more detailed in Mark 12:41}* we are introduced to a woman who gave her best. She gave her all. Jesus is standing by the offering plates watching

Living Generously / Giving Generously: The Spiritual Discipline of Stewardship

people put in their offerings.

Now isn't that a scary thought? What if Jesus stood by your church's offering plate and watched what each person put in? That is a scary thought! Well, in this Biblical passage Jesus is doing exactly that. Jesus notices that many rich people lined up. I suppose with great fanfare they placed their bags of gold in the offering box.

Jesus' disciples were standing there too. They also noticed all the large gifts being place in the offering too.

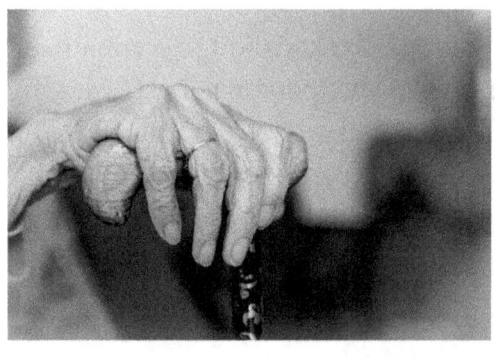

But then as they watched, a poor widow woman got in line. She was very poor, very poor indeed. When she got to the offering box, she emptied her purse into the offering box and two copper coins dropped in. Two pennies.

I imagine Jesus nudging his disciples saying, *"Hey fellas did you just see that? That poor widow just put more money in the offering than anyone else!"*

I imagine the disciples responded, *"No Jesus you are wrong. Didn't you see all those rich men dropping in gold? She just dropped in two pennies!"*

Jesus answered, *"I tell you that this poor woman put in more than all the others. For the others offered their gifts from what they had to spare of their riches; but she poor as she is, gave all she had to live on."*

The widow did her best. Her very best.

†††

There was a peanut farmer from Georgia who attended Georgia Tech, and then the Naval Academy. After getting out of the Naval Academy, he applied for the nuclear submarine program. In order to be admitted, he had to have a personal interview with Admiral Hyman Rickover.

President Jimmy Carter writes in his book, Why Not The Best? *"I had applied for the nuclear submarine program, and Admiral Rickover was interviewing me for the job. It was the first time I met Admiral Rickover. We were in a very large room for more than two hours... He began to ask me a series of questions of increasing difficulty. In each instance, he soon proved that I knew relatively little... He always looked right into my eyes, and he never smiled. I was saturated with cold sweat.*

Finally, he asked me a question and I thought I could redeem myself. He asked, 'How did you stand in your class at the Naval Academy?'

I swelled my chest with pride and answered, 'Sir, I stood fifty-ninth in a class of 820!' I sat back to wait for the congratulations - which never came.

Instead, he asked the question, 'Did you do your best?'

I started to say, 'Sir, yes, sir!' But then I... recalled several of the times when I could have learned more about our allies, our enemies, weapons, strategy... I finally gulped and answered, 'No sir, I did not always do my best.'

He looked at me for a long time, and then turned his chair around to end the interview. With his back toward me, he asked me one final question. I will never be able to forget it, or answer it, for that matter. He asked, 'Why not? Why not?'

I sat there for a while, shaken, and then slowly I left the room."

Did you do you best?

Why not?

†††

What God wants out of you and me, more than anything else, is that we offer to the Lord our very best. Not our second best. Not our third best. Not our fourth best, but our very best.

I wonder how many of us, can honestly say that we only offer the Lord our very best? Far too often, we say: *"I know I could do more, but I think I'll settle for this."*

We answer softly to ourselves: *"I've got more to give, but I think this will do, and besides, who will know the difference?"*

Or we think, *"I know the Lord calls me to do more, but I'm just human. He will understand."*

But then we hear the echo of Admiral Rickover's question: *"Did you do your best?"*

And we hear Jimmy Carter stumble around and answer, *'No sir, I did not always do my best.'*

And we hope God doesn't respond the way Admiral Rickover did, turning his back and asking, *"Why not? Why not?"*

†††

The Salvation Army is one of the largest charities in the country. It receives more dollars than St. Jude's Children's Hospital, American Red Cross, Habitat for Humanity, Good Will, or the American Cancer Society.

The Salvation Army raises right at 2 billion a year.

Do you know how it started? It began 125 years

ago in the slums of London, England, by a British Methodist preacher named William Booth. Years later, William Booth was asked how it all happened. Listen to his answer: *"It wasn't because of my talent and ability, because I am a very ordinary person. It wasn't because of my education, because I have only a very modest one. And certainly it's not because of any connections I have made, because I am just a very simple man. If anything, it's because I gave myself totally to the Lord. I told him he could have all there is of William Booth."*

That is the kind of people God is looking for.

People who will give all they've got.

People who offer the Lord their very best.

I wonder if God can count on you and me, to be among those who offer the Lord their very best?

And if we were to begin today striving to do our best, what would have to start changing at home, at work, and here in our hearts? I wonder?

†††

When I travelled to the Holy Land a couple of years ago, I couldn't help but notice the number of Jewish men who wore something like a small skull cap on their heads all the time. When we got close to a Jewish holy site, they would distribute these for all the men in our group to wear.

Norman Neeves got the courage to ask one of the Jewish men there in Jerusalem why they always wore the cap. Listen to the answer: *"I wear it all the time because I need to be reminded all the time that there's Someone who is over me and above me. I am not the Almighty. I am not the Lord. I'm just one of the many sheep in his pasture."* Isn't that a powerful statement? *"I wear it all the time because I need to be reminded all the time that there's Someone who is over me and above me. I am not the Almighty. I am not the Lord. I'm just one of the many sheep in his pasture."*

I wonder what it would mean in your life and in my life, if we lived with that attitude as well?

†††

Living Generously / Giving Generously: The Spiritual Discipline of Stewardship

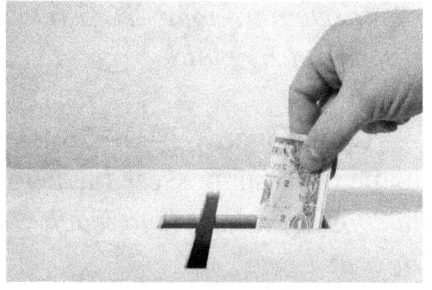

In the New Testament we find that Jesus never commanded the disciples to put 10% in the offering plate. The two percentages Jesus did commend, however, were far more than 10%. In Luke, Jesus commends Zacheaus' pledging to give 50% of his net worth. In Luke and Mark, Jesus commends the widow's example, because she emptied her savings and put in 100% of her financial resources.

†††

The idea of giving 10% is not a practical reduction of Jesus's commending 50% or 100%. Nor is the idea of giving 10% to God through the church just a cleaver fund rasing slogan. If you are wondering how much you should give, 10% is a rather biblical place to start.

†††

In dozens of places, the Old Testament is pretty clear about giving 10% of one's annual income back to God.

In Genesis 28:22 after a dream at Bethel, in gratitude Jacob says, *'I will surely give a tenth to God."*

In Malachi 3: 8-10 we read, *"Stop robbing God... Bring the full tithe..."*

In Deuteronomy 12:5-6, we read: *"bring ... your tithes and special gifts, and your freewill offerings..."*

Deuteronomy 14:22-29 teaches one tenth of all that comes into our possession, belongs to God, and that *"the purpose of tithing is to teach you to always put God first in your lives."*

Numbers 18:26 talks of presenting a tithe *"as the LORD's offering."*

In Matthew 23:23 Jesus states that tithing alone is not enough. We should also not neglect the more important issues of justice, mercy and faith.

†††

I invite you to give with joy and thanksgiving; to give with a smile on your face; to give out of gratitude; to give because you feel called by God to give; to give because you have prayed, "Lord, what would you do through me?"; and to give, because you want to give.

If you don't absorb anything else, let this one thing from II Corinthans 9: 6-7 sink in: ***"Each of you must give as you have made up your mind, not reluctantly or under compulsion, for God loves a cheerful giver!"*** (CEB) I get the impression that to the Apostle Paul, who wrote these ancient words, the Sunday morning offering plates were just as natural as singing hymns, reading scripture, or receiving the Lord's Supper.

Living Generously / Giving Generously: The Spiritual Discipline of Stewardship

For 4,000 years, the faithful have been called to set aside one-tenth of their annual income and return it to the Lord. Not 1/10th of the leftovers, but 1/10th of the first fruits. Tithing's historic Biblical purpose has been to always put God first in life.

We are not invited to give 10% to earn salvation, but rather to give 10% in grateful response to the salvation already received. We give in loving response to God's grace, not to earn it.

Today, 2000 years later, widows are still giving sacrificially. In many of our churches it is the widows who are sacrificially giving 10% of their social security and pension every Sunday. At the same time, far too many in the congregation, like those in line with the biblical widow, are only *"giving out of their spare change."* Luke 21: 4 (CEB)

†††

When it comes to stewardship and the church offering, what

would integrity look like?

Perhaps something like this:

• *Giving will be a priority in my life, growing to include the following:*

• *Giving will be the greatest joy in life.*

• *If I miss a week, I will give twice as much the next week to keep faith with my commitment.*

• *I will move closer to tithing (giving 10%) each year.*

• *The check or e-transfer to the church will be the first one I write each month.*

Jim Moore tells the story about a member of St. Luke's Church in Houston, Texas. Listen to what he says about her: *"Evie Jo Wilson is a really remarkable woman. She's had cancer and she's going through chemotherapy. She's almost 90 years old, but you'll never know it. And there's something else about Evie Jo that you should*

know. She's a reverse tither! When people tithe, they give 10% to the Lord and have 90% to live on. Evie Jo gives 90%, and keeps just 10% to live on! She's a reverse tither!"

Evie Joe Wilson herself said, *"Oh, it's so much fun! There's so much joy in it! Everything I give away I get to keep, but what I keep is what I lose."*

With a twinkle in her eye, she explains: *"What I keep doesn't bring joy to me at all. It just keeps me going... groceries... utility bills... It is the money I give away that brings me joy, and it keeps doing it forever and ever."*

Isn't that a great spirit? A wonderful attitude? There is a joy in generosity.

When we give to the church there should be no wrinkled brows, twisted arms, or gritted teeth. We should give out of joy and celebration.

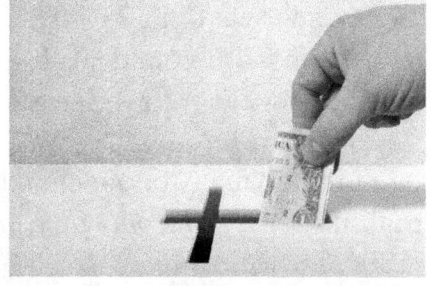

When you and I are faithful in our tithes and offerings, we are able to make ministry happen. Your local church has big dreams about children's ministry, youth ministry, local mission projects, and carrying the Gospel to the world. They believe God has called your church to do these things.

However, these things can not be done without your help. These things can not be done without each of us climbing one step in this commitment, growing closer to the Biblical minimum of giving the 10% tithe of our income through the church.

There is a great joy in giving, and in knowing that our gifts are making wonderful things happen.

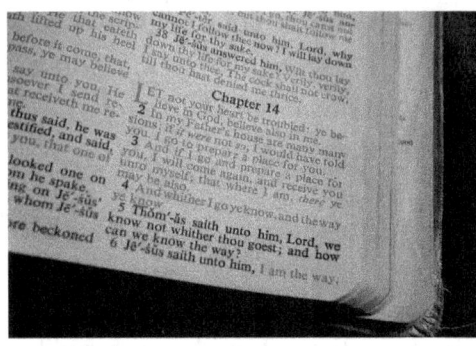

In his book *Consecration Sunday* Herb Miller has counted 500 verses in the Bible on prayer, 500 verses on faith, and more than 2,000 verses on money and what money buys. Jesus talked a lot about money, and I'm confident that the synagogue offering increased in every town Jesus taught in.

If far too many of our churches members can almost truthfully say, *"The only time my church thinks of me is when they want money."* or *"The only thing my church seems to want from me is my money."*

That isn't true, and should never be true. However, I can see why some members might get that impression. In far too many of our churches:

- the only time we send a first class letter is when it's about money;

- the only time we ask for a written commitment is when it's about money; and

- the only time we ask for a signature is when it's about money.

†††

"Tell them to use their money to do good. They should be rich in good works and should give happily to those in need, always being ready to share with others whatever God has given them. By doing this, they will be storing up real treasures for themselves in heaven. It is the only safe investment for eternity! And they will be living a fruitful Christian life down here as well." I Timothy 6: 18-19 (Living Bible)

Let us pray: *O Lord, once again it seems to be a matter of priorities. What do we want the most. Do we want to be rich on earth or to be rich in heaven? Do we want to be generous? Do we want to return to God a portion of our resources? Lord, help us to know what we should do with this invitation. In Jesus name.* Amen.

Focus Point

Years ago I attended a workshop with Hilbert Berger. He said, *"There is an existing contract of sorts with your existing members, and it is hard to change that old contract. It can be done slowly over time. However, with new members, you can offer them a revised contract, so to speak, and thoroughly train the new members how to follow it."*

Action Step: What are the expectations you have of new members of your congregation?

Action Step: If you were to list 12 expectations the Lord has of those who seek to be deeply devoted disciples, in addition to prayers, presence, gifts and service, what might those 12 be?

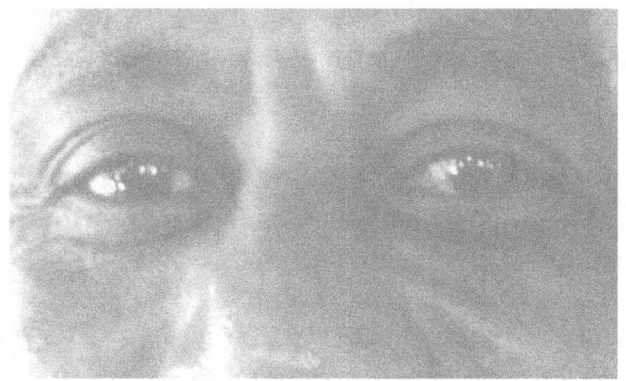

Chapter Two

You've just spent a few minutes working on a list of the expectations the Lord has for those who seek to become deeply devoted disciples.

What are several ways you might intentionally implant high expectation DNA into your local church?

How might you be honest with your congregation and reveal to them that the Lord expects a great deal more, than just our money?

To begin this process,

I suggest you design an intentional discipleship system. By *"discipleship system"* I am referring to a process, a method beyond the worship hour, for leading new inquirers into discipleship and then on to a deeply devoted discipleship.

Most new believers need **more** than just worship on Sunday to support and encourage their growth toward becoming deeply devoted disciples.

The old traditional system is still in place in most of our churches. It includes several facets.

First, is worship on Sunday morning.

Secondly, Sunday School for all ages.

Third, children's ministry. Perhaps an after school program on Wednesdays for older elementary and a membership or Confirmation Class for those in the sixth grade.

Fourth, youth ministry on Sunday evening. This is supplemented by a summer youth mission trip and perhaps church camp.

Fifth, a men's group that meets monthly.

Sixth, a monthly women's group.

In the United Methodist Church there is a **seventh**. In the 1980's we added a nine month class called "Disciple

Bible Study" written by Richard Wilke.

✝✝✝

How is that working for you?

In some locations this Discipleship System is working, but in many of our churches we are finding that this traditional Discipleship System just isn't leading new believers to become deeply devoted disciples who are faithfully on a journey toward prayers, presence, gifts, service, and witness.

If that is the situation in your congregation, as the pastor and lay leader, you have the opportunity to influence the congregation's understanding of discipleship by the content of your sermons, Bible studies, and devotionals at church council meetings.

I am NOT suggesting that you completely shut the old system down. Rather I am suggesting that you add additional support systems for new believers.

✝✝✝

Many of your current members joined under an "old contract" with very few expectations. It is difficult to renegotiate that old contract with your existing members. However, slowly over time, you can take the opportunity to invite your congregation to move toward becoming a more "high expectation church."

However, with prospective members, you can raise the bar of expectations rather quickly, and support them on that journey. Perhaps you do that by offering a Sunday evening monthly coffee with the pastor for worship guests. Maybe you also offer a newcomers class. In both of these sessions begin to give newcomers, the next wave of new members, a clearer image of what you understand the Lord expects of those who seek to become followers.

First, however, you need to decide what that "bar of expectations" is.

I invite you to decide exactly:

- What is a deeply devoted disciple?

- What does Jesus Christ expect of faithful followers?

- What fruit?

- What holy habits?

- What works of mercy?

- What works of piety does the Lord expect in the lives of the faithful?

Your answer should be reflected in the content of the sermons, Bible studies, devotionals, church council meetings, and the process you offer households seeking to make your church their "home."

Focus Point

In many of Craig Miller's workshops he has offered a Spiritual Leader's Checklist. I've adapted his checklist below. Take a few minutes to answer these check lists. Then, if you are in a group studying this book, at the end of the last check list, share any insights you've had with each other.

Spiritual Life of the Leader

As a pastor or lay leader you are creating the normative expectations for spiritual growth in your congregation. Your prayer life, physical health, artistic pursuits, and relationships have a direct influence on the spiritual life of your congregation's leaders. What experiences sustain you and connect you to God and others?

What is YOUR plan for YOUR personal continued spiritual growth and development?

- How do you connect with God?
  - __ Day apart
  - __ Worship
  - __ Family prayer
  - __ Meeting with a prayer partner
  - __ Daily devotional time
  - Other: _____
- How are you connecting with others?
  - __ Time alone with spouse or friend
  - __ I've set aside a specific day or evening to spend with my family
  - __ Focused time with your children
  - __ Regular connection with extended family

___ Time with friends outside of church
Other: _____
- What arts feed your soul?
  ___ Writing
  ___ Playing musical instrument/singing
  ___ Dance
  ___ Drawing
  ___ Gardening
Other: _____
- How are you taking care of your body?
  ___ Walking/running
  ___ Active in a sport
  ___ Healthy diet
  ___ Aerobics
Other: _____

†††

Personal Spiritual Leader Checklist
Reflect on the John Wesley's Means of Grace (¶72, The UM Book of Discipline).
Wesley's Means of Grace include:
- Public worship of God
- Christian conferencing
- Receiving the Lord's Supper
- Family and private prayer
- Searching the Scriptures
- Fasting or abstinence
- The Bible either read or preached.

Based on these means of grace,
complete the **Spiritual Leader Checklist** below:
*Complete the following survey,
giving yourself 10 points for each 'yes' answer.*

Yes or No

_____ 1. I say grace before each meal.

_____ 2. I set aside a time to pray each day

_____ 3. At least once a week, I pray out loud with another person *(a family member, a friend, a person at work or church).*

_____ 4. I read at least one verse of Scripture every day.

_____ 5. I attend worship at our church at least three times a month.

_____ 6. At least twice a month I meet with a group of people to pray, reflect on Scripture, and build one another up *(in a small group, Sunday school class, prayer group, etc.)*

_____ 7. I take Holy Communion at least once a month.

_____ 8. At least once a month I give of myself to others. *(I volunteer at a homeless shelter or soup kitchen, visit in a nursing home, tutor a child, visit a prisoner, mow a neighbor's lawn, etc.)*

_____ 9. I fast once a week *(I give up food for a period of time or do a media fast and go without electronic media – TV, radio, etc. – for a day.)*

_____ 10. I tithe at least 10% of my income through my church.

_____ 11. As part of every meeting at church, we spend 10-15 minutes praying together and reflecting on a Scripture passage.

_____ **TOTAL POINTS**
(ten points for each 'yes')

Spiritual Expectations Checklist
For Your Church's Leaders

Central to the life of any congregation is its leadership. What happens in the church's leadership team *(Sunday school teachers, small group leaders, elected members of boards and committees, and staff)* affects the life of the whole congregation.

What spiritual disciplines will your church's leadership team be expected to practice?

__ Weekly worship
__ Daily Bible reading
__ Service to others
__ Fasting or abstinence
__ Family Prayer
__ Daily Prayer
__ Receive the Lord's Supper
  __weekly; __monthly
__ Tithing 10% of their income through the church
__ Other: _____

Living Generously / Giving Generously: The Spiritual Discipline of Stewardship

††††

You've had a few minutes to reflect on what the Lord might expect of those who seek to be deeply devoted disciples. The question now is, *"How do you invite your leadership team to join same journey you've you've experienced while reading this book?"*

There is a resource written by Junius Dotson that will do exactly that. It is provided by the United Methodist Church and you can download it for free at: www.SeeAllThePeople.org

Junius Dotson's book is a great resource filled discussion starters for your leadership team.

It is filled with ideas for intentionally allowing space for Prevenient Grace, Justifying Grace, and Sanctifying Grace to be at work in your congregation.

It is filled with ideas for people

who are at five different levels of Christian maturity: exploring, searching, beginning, growing, and maturing levels.

It is filled with ideas for worship, community, spiritual practice, generosity, service, and living a Christ-like lifestyle.

In the process of working with your team, I encourage you to end up with a simple diagram, in English – not church language – so that newcomers can easily understand the journey you are inviting them to begin.

For example, Ben Anderson at Woodlands Church in Fort Smith has developed this Discipleship System and chart.

It is prominently displayed in the lobby, and simply outlines for first-time worship guest the discipleship path they are invited to take.

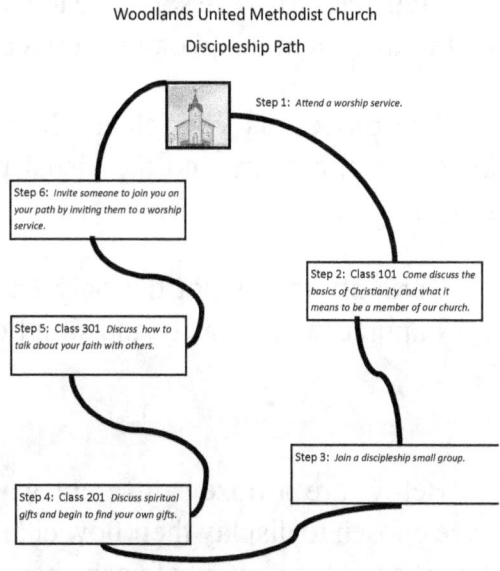

Step one is to attend worship.

Step two is to attend "Class 101" to discuss the books of Christianity and what it means to be a member of the church.

Step three is to join a discipleship small group.

Step four is "Class 201" to discuss spiritual gifts and begin to find your own gifts.

Step five is "Class 301" to discuss how to talk about your faith with others.

Step six is to invite someone to join you on your path by inviting them to a worship service.

The process is very clear. Religious language is kept to a minimum, and the visual poster is simple to follow.

Certainly this is not the only Discipleship System, but I appreciate its clarity and simplicity.

†††

Below are a dozen different ways local churches have chosen to display their flow chart. For our purpose now it's not the content of each chart - but the variety of imagery local churches have chosen.

Living Generously / Giving Generously: The Spiritual Discipline of Stewardship

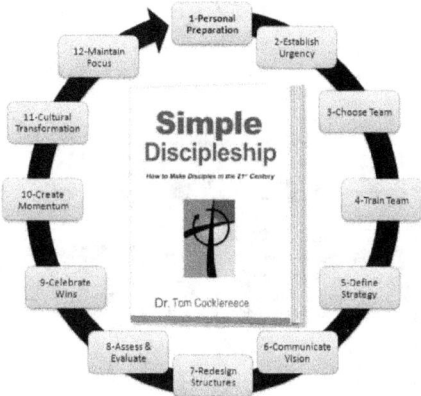

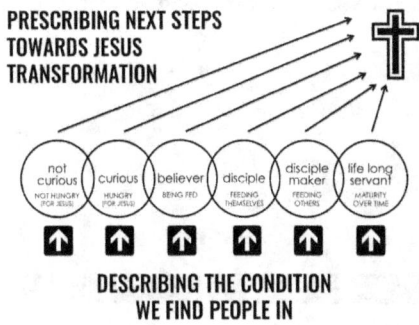

Living Generously / Giving Generously: The Spiritual Discipline of Stewardship

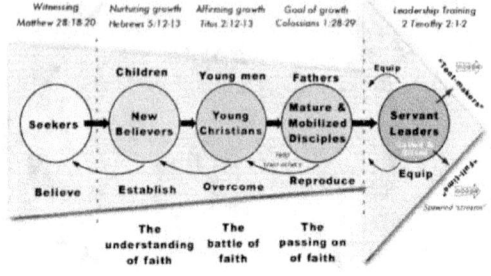

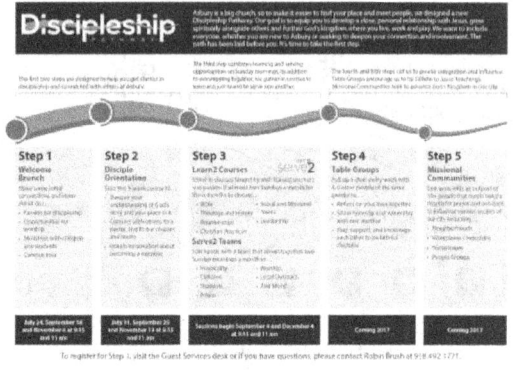

Living Generously / Giving Generously: The Spiritual Discipline of Stewardship

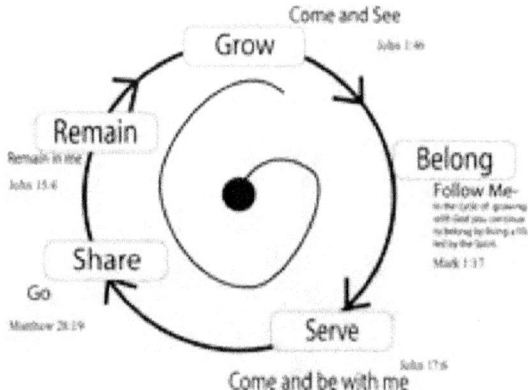

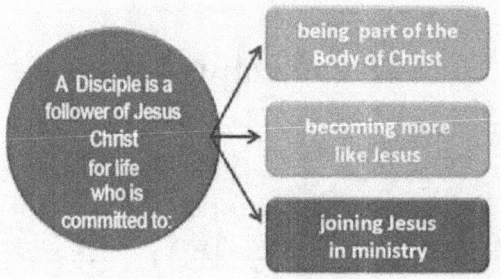

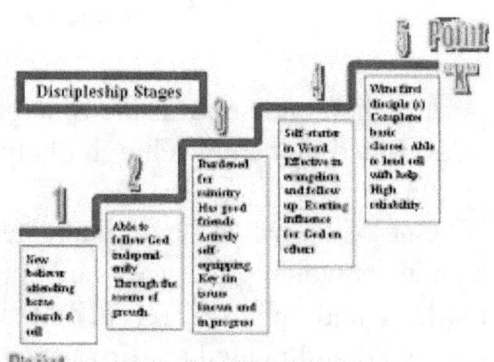

The point at which a disciple carries on independently with other disciples. My efforts have been "duplicated."

– 47 –

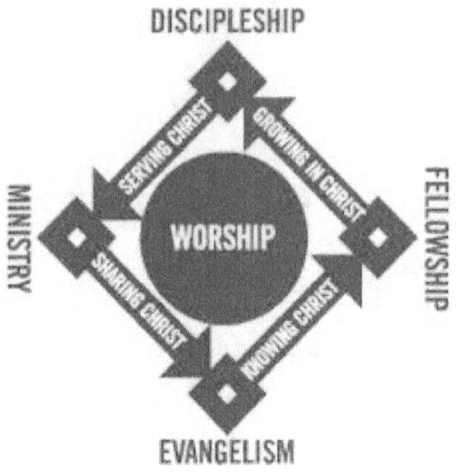

Discipleship Process

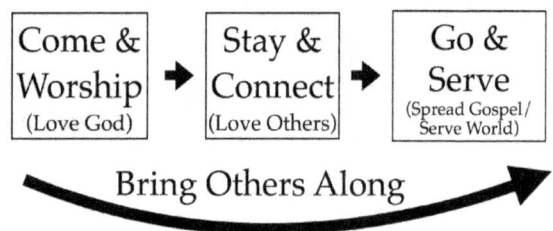

The diamond below is the Discipleship System chart I developed in the new church I helped to launch.

One of the ways I communicated this Discipleship System to worship guest was by email and by physical mail. I had seven different letters that a volunteer addressed and mailed the first seven times a household was a worship guest.

Living Generously / Giving Generously: The Spiritual Discipline of Stewardship

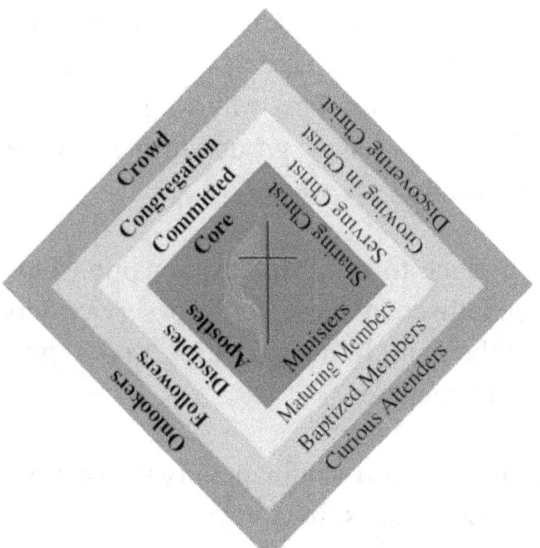

Steps of Commitment... A New Testament Pattern

Each letter introduced and invited the new household to participate in a different facet or ministry of the church.

All seven letters had one thing in common – it included this flow chart, and an insert that listed the steps in simple language.

1. To move from the fringes to the core of this congregation, begin to develop the holy habit of attending worship every week.

2. Begin to pray every day. Listen to the prayer time on Sundays, and take the printed prayer list home with you each week. You might also want to use the Upper Room booklet provided free in our lobby each month.

3. Find a small group for Christian support and growth. We have found here at Grace Church that small groups are the best way to grow as a Christian. There is a list of groups printed in the worship handout every week.

4. Find a place to serve in Jesus' name. On the main bulletin board there is a list of service opportunities at the church, mission trips, and a list of United Way agencies.

5. Begin to be generous, financially supporting the work of Jesus Christ in Conway.

6. Begin to invite your family, friends, neighbors, and co-workers to join you here at Grace on Sundays.

7. Attend *"Coffee with the Pastor"* offered at 7pm on the first Sunday evening of each month.

8. Attend "Grace Basics" offered at 7pm on the second Sunday evening of each month.

9. After all of these, you may be ready for the vows of membership, to officially make Grace Church your home.

✝✝✝

Let me add a footnote here:

A healthy church has dozens or hundreds of people at each level. As people move toward the core, a new generation of the curious must be found.

A church that says, *"Let's get rid of the deadbeats! We want only deeply devoted disciples in this church!"* – that is a church that is going to die.

The people on the fringes are not deadbeats. Rather, they are your next wave of new believers, they are your hope, and they are your future.

A typical congregation looses about 10% of it's active participants every year. They are lost through funerals, admission to a nursing home, retired couples moving to be closer to their children, company transfers, and a few households who just drift away.

Without a continual stream of new people on the fringes, in five to ten years your church will lose vitality and strength. Your church will be saying, *"In the past we had to have two worship services on Sunday morning to hold everyone. In the past we had a choir, youth group, a nursery, and three women's circles. In the past we had a full-time pastor..."*

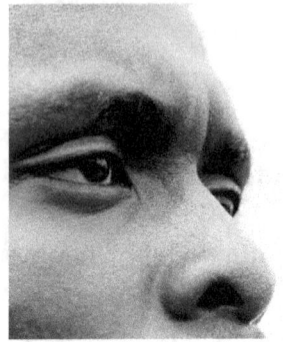

Focus Point

Where does financial stewardship fit in?

What financial expectations does the Lord have of his faithful followers?

What I want to propose to you is that in far too many of our churches the expectations are: prayers, presence, **GIFTS**, service, and witness.

In far too many of our local churches, the only time a first class letter is sent to the congregation is when it's about money.

The only time a signature is requested is when it's about money.

The only *"annual campaign"* is about money.

In far too many of our churches, the nominal attendee can almost say with honesty, *"You know it seems like the only thing my church wants from me is my money."*

That should never be the case.

We know that isn't true. We know the Lord expects a great deal from those who seek to be deeply devoted disciples of Jesus Christ.

Action Step: In groups of two and three, brainstorm ways you might begin to communicate "prayers, presence, gifts, service, witness, reading the Bible, forgiveness – IN EQUAL MEASURE to your congregation.

†††

Living Generously / Giving Generously: The Spiritual Discipline of Stewardship

Chapter Three

I want to share with you the discipleship system I developed in response to the issues we've been discussing up to now.

Perhaps you can take this basic idea, as you strengthen the discipleship system in your local church, and design your own system that uniquely fits your congregation.

When Clif Christopher recommended my program in one of his books, the Methodist Publishing House gave me a call and asked for a copy. The next week they called and said, *"Can you come to Nashville, we need to talk."* A few months later they published my program as the recommended annual Discipleship Education system for the United Methodist Church that year. It's been used by hundreds of our congregations across the country.

You don't need to buy my program. You can take these basic ideas, and design your own.

Here is the story of how I developed my discipleship system.

†††

I was the pastor of a new church. The church was only five years old. We had grown from an initial group of 40 to 400 in worship. I had witnessed 200 professions of faith, 100 reaffirmations of faith, more than 200 baptisms, and a church family of over 1,000 people. We had also witnessed transfers of membership from over 250 congregations representing 23 different denominations.

It was time for the church to step up to the next level, but I had two concerns:

First, my discipleship system was weak and out of focus.

I had a congregation filled with new believers. However most of the congregation did not have a clear, articulate, or compelling sense of exactly what the Lord expected of them as disciples.

About a fifth of the adults in the church had participated in the nine month *"Disciple Bible Study: Becoming Disciples Through Bible Study"* written by Richard Wilke. A smaller number of the Disciple graduates had also completed the second and third year of that amazing program.

However, if asked, *"Tell me what the Lord expects of those who seek to be faithful disciples?"* The response from the typical congregant would either be a blank stare, rambling thoughts, or a lengthy attempt to summarize what they had learned in *Disciple Bible Study*.

The congregation did not have a focused, clear, articulate, or compelling sense of what the Lord expected of them as disciples. As pastor of this fast-growing congregation, I was concerned that a significant number in the church family were not fully engaged in a journey toward becoming deeply devoted disciples of Jesus Christ.

Secondly, I was the only paid staff. You might say that I was the Senior pastor, Associate Pastor, Chaplain, Teaching Pastor, Youth Minister,

Children's Minister, Church Administrator, Church Secretary, Church Custodian, and Lawn Care guy.

I did have volunteers. I had 200 volunteers, but I was the contact person. I was juggling, training, and coordinating those 200 volunteers. It was exhausting, but it was working.

However, I knew if we were going to **hold on to** our 1,000 people, and **keep making more** new disciples - the system had to change.

I believed it was time for the church to begin adding program and support staff.

That year we added our first paid staff in office, music and children's ministry which increased the church's operating budget by $50,000.

However, the offering only showed a modest increase that spring. We had a shortfall of $1,000 every Sunday. We were headed toward a $50,000 deficit for the year. A slow motion financial train wreck was happening in front of my eyes.

I knew the system needed to change. I knew we had to increase our financial resources to meet the growing ministry. I traveled to Oklahoma City to visit my friend Dr. Norman Neaves, founding pastor of Church of the Servant.

Living Generously / Giving Generously: The Spiritual Discipline of Stewardship

Norman had been our consultant, so it didn't take long to describe the new financial train wreck that was happening with a $1,000 short fall each Sunday.

His reply was simple, *"Tell me about your stewardship program."*

I answered, *"Oh, we do about the same or more than most churches. We emphasize financial stewardship during the first two weeks of November. A letter is mailed to the membership with an enclosed pledge card. The following Sunday the Church Treasurer speaks for a few minutes from the pulpit, asking everyone to take the card home and to pray about their decision. He then invites the congregation to bring the card back the next week. My sermon that Sunday is on the subject of giving."*

After a long pause, Dr. Neaves asked, *"Is that all?"*

My puzzled look in response revealed volumes to Dr. Neaves.

Norman began to share with me his understanding of stewardship. He said that our task as pastors is to invite the congregation, and the mission field that surrounds it, to not only accept Jesus Christ as Lord and Savior, but to grow each year toward becoming deeply devoted disciples of Jesus Christ.

He went on to share that he was looking for an annual way to begin inviting his congregation, step by step, to join in that journey.

He believed that the commitments should involve prayers, presence in worship, financial gifts, and service. He also believed that the Lord called each of us to journey closer and closer to the cross, and to also reach back to invite others to join us in that journey.

After visiting with Norman, driving for six hours back to my home in Conway – the *Committed to Christ* stewardship program was born.

As I drove home, several personal experiences shaped my thoughts.

I remembered when my parents began to give sacrificially. They were about 40 years old and I was in elementary school. My family was active at St. Matthew's in Houston, Texas.

That church began a ten year emphasis on giving. The invitation was rather simple: *"If you do not currently support the church financially, begin this year giving 2% of your income to the church. If you are currently giving 2% of your income, begin this year growing just one step to 3%. Wherever you are in this journey, grow just one step each year 4, 5, 6, 7, 8, 9% until you have reached that Biblical standard of the 10% tithe."*

If I remember correctly, my parents were giving about 4% at the time. That year our family made a commitment that we would grow one step each year – and we did exactly that.

I say, "we" because such a decision to make the tithe a priority affects the whole family. With my parents giving more money to the church, there was less disposable income for the minor luxuries my brother and I were used to.

Also, my brother and I began to tithe our allowance and any money we earned by raking leaves or mowing lawns for neighbors.

A second experience reinforced my childhood memories of tithing.

At the age of eighteen, a life changing moment happened to me my first summer as a youth minister. Brother I.L. Claude was a saintly retired pastor in that church. In his youth, he rode horseback to travel along his circuit of churches. He crossed rivers and built a fire on the other side to dry his clothes. He slept many a night under the stars.

Brother Claude knew I was going to Hendrix College and that I was in training to be the pastor of a church. While we were standing in his front yard, he offered me one bit of advice to build my ministry on. He invited me to decide, at the tender age of 18, who was Lord of my life. It was one of those Life-changing – God moments in my life. Brother Claude put it this way, *"Give the first 10% of your paycheck back to God. The second 10% is for savings and investments toward retirement. And live on the 80% that remains."*

He added, *"I've done that all my life."* He turned and motioned toward his home behind us, and said, *"I have been faithful to God, and God has been faithful to me, and blessed me beyond my wildest hopes."*

My income at the time was $75 a week. Brother Claude invited me to put $7.50 in saving, $7.50 in the offering, and to live on the remaining $60.

My wife and I have strived to be faithful to those guidelines for forty years.

What a great joy it has been. The 80% we kept has disappeared to pay bills.

But the 10% we gave to the church, is still enriching the lives of children and youth, is still working through our missionaries overseas, and is still providing buildings for worship of the Lord.

For some people, this idea of giving does **not** come natural. The idea of placing **any** money in the offering plate is a difficult thought. A very difficult thought.

Most of us struggle with the insatiable desire for more. We desire more money and what money buys. We want bigger houses, nicer cars, more clothes, longer vacations and nicer vacations. We want more of everything.

The love of money and the love of what money can buy is putting marriages at risk, and affecting their future.

Driven to spend more than they have, the "Visa bill from hell" each month is robbing our church members of the joy of life and certainly robbing them of the joy of giving back to God.

†††

Driving home from Oklahoma City, I wondered, *"How can I invite the members of my church to begin the journey toward the 10% tithe?"*

I also thought about other areas of discipleship.

My personal journey – all of the times the Lord continued to invite me to take another step closer, and to live more faithfully as one of his disciples.

I wish I could report that I have completed the

journey. I have not. I am not perfect. I still sin. I fall short of the goal that Christ has placed in front of me. There have been seasons when I have said, *"Lord, just leave me alone. I've grown in the faith all I care to grow right now."*

But thank God, the Lord has not left me alone. As the hymn says, the Lord continued to *"walk with me and talk with me."*

The Lord invited me to continue the journey toward daily prayer, reading the Bible daily, faithful worship attendance, to be winsome in my witness, financial giving growing to the Biblical minimum standard of the ten percent tithe, and giving my time to serve others in Jesus' name.

One month, it seems that I've taken three steps forward, and then the next month it seems like I've taken four steps backward. And yet, by God's Grace, as the months go by, overall I've travelled forward. I've changed. I've been molded by the very Spirit of God.

✝✝✝

Driving home from Oklahoma City I thought of all these experiences in my personal life, and I wondered – *"How can I invite the members of my church to begin taking steps like these – steps toward Holy Living – steps toward Sanctification!"*

The pieces began to come together.

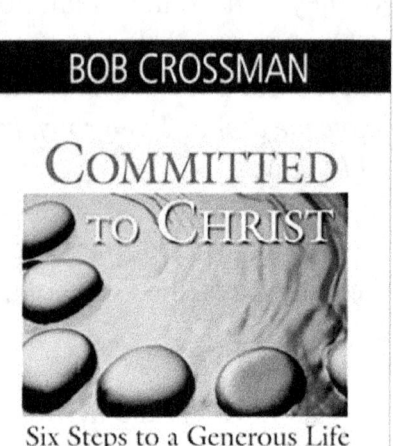

Over the next six months, I designed a strategy to invite my local church to begin a journey, step by step, across a broad spectrum of discipleship.

Implementing the basic plan of *"Committed to Christ: Six Steps to a Generous Life,"* within a year, the number of pledging households in my church increased by 17%, the amount pledged increased 58%, and the actual offering receipts grew by 64%.

The vitality of the church surged forward as commitments were made and commitments were kept. The church became engaged in the journey and insisted the program be repeated year after year as they continued to grow, and step up toward becoming deeply devoted disciples.

†††

What I designed is a holistic discipleship education emphasis which places financial giving

Living Generously / Giving Generously: The Spiritual Discipline of Stewardship

within the context of what the Lord expects of those who seek to be faithful disciples of the Lord.

It is NOT simply an annual financial campaign for the local church.

The focus is not on the church's needs, but rather upon each individual's need to respond generously to the saving Grace of Jesus Christ - with their hearts and with their hands.

This is the program that the United Methodist Publishing House, through Abingdon Press, adopted as the Annual Stewardship Program for the United Methodist Church that year.

✝✝✝

In far too many annual stewardship campaigns, the truth is that the pastor and the church office take care of the entire program. They only need to recruit a lay person who will agree for their signature to be on the congregational letter and maybe to speak about the pledge cards for two minutes one Sunday.

In contrast, the *"Committed to Christ: Six Steps to a Generous Life"* program begins when a steward team (or teams) is chosen, along with a Celebration  Team to lead this six week emphasis. The entire team will be invited to lead by making advance commitments in all six areas. The team will divide into half a dozen work groups to make the different facets of the program happen. THIS IS A CRITICAL PIECE, AND IT CAN NOT BE OVEREMPHASIZED.

†††

One of the initial steps is to conduct a confidential survey in the congregation.

In each of these six areas of discipleship, the multiple choice survey asks (for example) not only about 'the frequency of  prayer, but also about the quality of their prayer life. A sample of the survey is printed below:

Living Generously / Giving Generously: The Spiritual Discipline of Stewardship

Confidential Survey

This survey form is to be completed by every adult in worship.
NO NAMES, PLEASE
This survey will be in our bulletin for several weeks.
Just fill the form out ONE time.

I was **BORN** between: __ 1990-2012   __ 1969-1989   __ 1948-1968
                        __ 1927-1947   __ 1900-1926

My **sex** is: __ Male   __ Female

My **marital status** is: __ Married   __ Single

Number of **PEOPLE IN MY CAR** this morning ____

Number of **MILES** I drive/commute to **CHURCH** ____

My home is: __North   __South   __East   __West of the church

Number of **MILES** I drive/commute to **WORK** ____

What **"MUSIC"** do I listen to the most?
  __Country   __Christian   __Rap
  __Easy Listening   __Classical   __Jazz
  __News/Talk   __Hard Rock   __Soft Rock
  __1950's-60's Music   __Children's   __Silence
  __National Public Radio __Books on Tape

MAGAZINE I read the most?: _____

I read the **CHURCH NEWSLETTER** every time: __Yes   __No

I use **E-MAIL** or **INTERNET** regularly: __Yes   __No

I am a: __ 1st or 2nd time Visitor   __ Continuing Guests   __Member

Our household **ANNUAL INCOME** is:
  __ less than 7,500   __7,500 to 14,999   __15,000 to 24,999
  __25,000 to 34,999   __35,000 to 49,999   __50,000 to 74,999
  __75,000 to 99,999   __100,000 to 124,999 __125,000 and up

In a **typical MONTH**,
  I PRAY ____ times a month
  I GIVE $_____ to God each month
  I GIVE _____ HOURS to God each month
  I read the BIBLE ____ times a month
  I attend WORSHIP ____ times a month
  I attend SUNDAY SCHOOL ____ times a month
  I WITNESS about God ____ times a month

I FIRST VISITED this Church because of:
  __ Friend   __ Door hanger invite   __ Newspaper invite

  __ Relative   __ Attractive Building   __ Yellow Page listing
  __ Live Nearby   __ Church Web Site   __ Telephone solicitation
  __ Co-Worker   __ _____

I CAME BACK to this Church because: _____

_____

I have been **ATTENDING** this church for ____ years OR ____ months.

Do you PRAY?
  ____ No, I have never prayed.
  ____ Yes, but only when facing difficult times.
  ____ Yes, I pray about once a week, usually in worship.
  ____ Yes, I pray five times a week.
  ____ Yes, I have a daily prayer routine that I faithfully carry out.
  ____ Yes, and I will continue to grow in my daily prayer life.

  Which of these apply to your PRAYER life?
    __ I pray, but the time seems empty and I wonder if God listens.
    __ All significant decisions I make are preceded by prayer.
    __ When I pray, I sometimes truly feel God's presence.
    __ Prayer has become my constant companion, my joy unspeakable.
    __ Prayer is a central part of my daily life.

Living Generously / Giving Generously: The Spiritual Discipline of Stewardship

Have you accepted JESUS CHRIST as your Lord & Savior?
___ No, I do not think I ever have accepted Jesus Christ.
___ No, but maybe someday.
___ No, but I want to with all my heart.
___ Yes, I have accepted Jesus Christ.
___ Yes, and SOMEDAY I will be ready for an even closer walk.

Which of these apply to your relationship with JESUS CHRIST?
___ Jesus is the guide & constant companion of my life.
___ I sometimes ask, 'What would Jesus have me do?'
___ I always ask and obey, 'What would Jesus have me do?'
___ I feel that He walks with me daily.
___ I have a relationship with Christ, but not a very strong one.
___ I don't know. I wonder if it's possible to have such a relationship.

Do you support the Lord's church with your presence in WORSHIP?
___ I attend worship about three to six times a year.
___ I attend worship about once a month.
___ I attend worship about twice a month.
___ I attend worship about three times a month.
___ I attend worship about four times a month.
___ I almost never miss, even when out of town, I find a church.

Which of these apply to your WORSHIP life?
___ I truly look forward to, and anticipate worshipping God.
___ I arrive at church prepared: I've prayed and confessed my sins.
___ I don't simply observe, but I fully participate in the experience.
___ I experience God's presence in worship.
___ I find the strength, power, and direction to face the week ahead.

Do you support the Lord's church financially?
___ No.
___ On the average, I give $_____ each week to the General Fund.
___ On the average, I give $_____ each week to the Building Fund.
These gifts probably represent _____% of my income.

Living Generously / Giving Generously: The Spiritual Discipline of Stewardship

When you give money to support the Lord's church...
___ Giving is the greatest joy in my life.
___ The church check is the first one I write each month.
___ I am moving closer to tithing (10%) each year to honor God.
___ If I miss a Sunday, I give twice as much the next week.
___ I am growing closer to God through my giving.
___ I give, but not much.
___ I give financially, but I'm not sure why.
___ I give - if I happen to have a $1 or $5 bill in my wallet.
___ I probably waste more money each week than I give.

Do you witness, or tell others about your faith in the Lord?
___ No, I have never told anyone about my faith.
___ No, but maybe someday.
___ No, but I want to with all my heart.
___ Yes, sometimes.
___ Yes, frequently.
___ Yes, daily.
___ Yes, and I will continue to look for new opportunities to tell others.

Which of these apply to your witnessing life?
__ I regularly invite people to attend worship with me.
__ I regularly pray for the salvation of specific non-Christian people.
__ I share my faith, but I'm not sure how effective I am.
__ I am intentionally hoping for the opportunity to share with my non-Christian friends.
__ People have accepted Christ after I've shared by faith.
__ I continue those relationships, to offer the support they need.
__ I usually witness to:
   __ friends; __ relatives; __ neighbors; __ business associates

When you witness, what kind of witnessing do you do?
__ I invite people to attend worship at our Church.
__ I invite people to attend Sunday School with me.
__ I don't say much, but I believe my life-style and attitudes are a witness since they know I am doing these in Jesus' name.

Living Generously / Giving Generously: The Spiritual Discipline of Stewardship

___ When I witness, I use my Bible to explain the plan of salvation.
___ I often engage non-believers in deep theological discussions about sin, forgiveness, and the nature of Christ.
___ I look for opportunities to say, *"My faith in Jesus Christ has made all the difference in my life."*

Do you read the BIBLE?
___ No, I have never read the Bible.
___ No, I don't read the Bible, but I want to with all my heart.
___ I used to, but I don't anymore.
___ Yes, sometimes I read the Bible.
___ Yes, I frequently read the Bible.
___ Yes, I read the Bible on a daily schedule.

Which of these apply to your BIBLE reading life?
___ I have a hard time, the words just seem like words.
___ I am blessed and my faith is strengthened each time.
___ I sometimes think God has written it just for me.
___ I evaluate my ideas to see if they are consistent with the Bible.
___ Bible reading is one of the highlights of my life and faith.

Do you serve the Lord with your HANDS?
___ No, I've never given any time to serve God.
___ Yes, I do give my time, but only when directly asked to.
___ Yes, I take the initiative, searching for opportunities.
___ Yes, about one hour a week.
___ Yes, about three hours a week.
___ Yes, about five hours a week.
___ Yes, I give time to serve God every single day.
___ Yes, I give a tithe (10%) of my time to serve the Lord.

When I give my time to serve the Lord...
___ I feel closer to the Lord afterward.
___ I feel that my spiritual life is stronger.
___ I believe I have obeyed the Lord's command.
___ I feel a calling to do even more than I have.

I would VOLUNTEER at the church more...
__ If I knew they needed me.
__ If I were directly asked to volunteer
__ If it was only two hours a week, I just can't give 10 hours weekly.
__ If I knew I could rotate off after six months.
__ If I knew exactly what was expected.

I STOPPED VOLUNTEERING years ago because...
__ My employment responsibilities changed.
__ My home/parenting responsibilities changed.
__ My health changed.
__ I didn't feel appreciated or recognized for all my hard work.
__ I didn't feel that I was really making any difference.
__ _____

_____

Is there anything else you want to share?

_____

_____

_____

This survey was printed front and back of a single sheet of paper, and folded in half like a tall booklet. We placed a copy in each chair every Sunday for an entire month. I would say, *"In your chair is a confidential survey. Please do not put your name on it. If you have not already, complete the survey and place it in the offering plate today, or you can take it home and bring it with you next week.*

†††

Another initial step is to recruit laity to give a personal testimony each of the seven Sundays.

These are not to be "mini sermons" but testimonies. In the materials published by Abingdon Press, I included sample testimonies, because too many laity think they are being invited to give a mini-sermon. There is a difference between a mini-sermon and a testimony.

THIS IS A CRITICAL PIECE, AND IT CAN NOT BE OVEREMPHASIZED.

†††

Sermons are prepared in advance to match the theme of the introductory Sunday and each of the six Sundays that follow.

Abingdon Press developed a DVD included in the kit with worship loops for churches that use screens.

†††

Communication is put in place to take advantage of the pulpit, worship bulletin, bulletin boards, web site, facebook, blog, twitter, and any other social media your congregation uses.

†††

There are seven different commitment cards. Each one emphasized on a different Sunday with EQUAL emphasis.

THIS IS A CRITICAL PIECE. SEVEN CARDS - DON'T COMBINE INTO A SINGLE CARD. WE FIELD TESTED, AND THAT IS A MISTAKE.

This set is mailed to the congregation at the beginning, and then the appropriate card is placed on each chair on the Sunday it is being emphasized. A second set it mailed at the end with an invitation to catch up any Sundays they missed.

Living Generously / Giving Generously: The Spiritual Discipline of Stewardship

✝✝✝

There is also a stair step brochure that gives an overview of all six steps along with an invitation to climb one or more steps in each area of discipleship. This brochure is mailed to the entire church family and provided on every chair during the six week emphasis.

✝✝✝

Publicly, the emphasis begins with an introductory sermon and worship service focusing on making or reaffirming a commitment to Jesus Christ.

I actually suggest that you take two or three Sundays to introduce the journey.

In those introductory Sundays, you offer an invitation to be fully engaged: no more luke-warm disciples but to be hot for the Gospel; to get off the fence; and to join the journey toward becoming a deeply devoted disciple.

It is an invitation to journey together, toward Sanctification and Holy Living – a lifestyle that the Lord expects of faithful disciples.

During each of the following six weeks, this program offers a six-step method for building and strengthening that commitment to Christ through worship, small groups, and other activities. With each step, people will be asked to think seriously about and set goals for that particular aspect of discipleship. The six steps begin with interior activities and move outward.

I actually suggest that the first time you spend 2, 3 or 4 Sundays on each of the six steps.

†††

Let's look at the 6 steps or commitments:

During this first formal week, *"Committed to Christ"* invites each household to *"climb one or more steps"* in their journey toward having a deeply devoted **prayer life**.

This first step is about prayer, how prayer can transform life, and what prayer is really all about. We begin with prayer because if the people of your congregation are going to have a personal relationship with the Lord, it is going to begin with prayer.

This is not a step toward earning one's salvation, but rather a step toward a generous life in response to salvation already received from Christ.

The invitations on this Sunday are directed toward the new believer as well as the mature disciple. The invitations focus in part on the FREQUENCY of prayer, but also on the QUALITY of their prayer life.

†††

During this second formal week, *"Committed to Christ"* invites each household to *"climb one or more steps"* in their journey toward the holy habit of hearing, reading and reflecting on the holy words of scripture found in **the Bible**.

†††

During this third formal week, *"Committed to Christ"* invites each household to *"climb one or more steps"*

in their journey toward **faithful worship attendance**.

†††

During this fourth formal week, *"Committed to Christ"* invites each household to *"climb one or more steps"* in their journey toward being a faithful witness by **inviting others** to join this journey toward a commitment to Christ.

The Lord calls each of us to journey closer and closer to the cross, but also calls each of us to reach back and invite others to join us in this journey.

†††

During this fifth formal week, *"Committed to Christ"* invites each household to *"climb one or more steps"* in their **financial giving** to the church - to begin growing TOWARD the Biblical minimum standard of the ten percent tithe.

The commitment card for this week invites each individual to write in the exact amount of their commitment and to indicate if they are committing to give weekly, monthly, quarterly or yearly. There is also a space for them to indicate whether this is a ten percent tithe, or what percentage this amount represents.

†††

During this sixth formal week, *"Committed to Christ"* invites each household to *"climb one or more steps"* in their journey toward **service** – giving their time and abilities, to serve in Jesus' name, and to get blisters for Jesus.

Also on the sixth Sunday, a **Ministry Celebration** is held. Ministry Celebration Sunday is an exciting and compelling way to tell the church's story of ministries available, service opportunities, and changed lives utilizing a procession of ministry banners and display tables representing the ministries of your church.

Living Generously / Giving Generously: The Spiritual Discipline of Stewardship

†††

In addition to emails, blogs, website, newsletter and twitter invitations - TELEPHONE CALLS are also made by the Celebration Team to every household in the church family to encourage attendance for this Sunday.

The Celebration Team may also decide to have a Thanksgiving theme Celebration Luncheon on this 6th Sunday as well.

†††

During the Year With NEW Households

For the first three years - in my mission field, I made a door step visit at 12:30 every Sunday to that morning's worship guests. Also, new guest each month were invited to my home for a hamburger cookout. Following Adam Hamilton's pattern, after their third visit to worship I called and made a formal appointment to visit in their home.

In that home visit my message was: "We are a HIGH EXPECTATION CHURCH – we expect our members to..." I walked them through the seven cards and gave them an eighth family information card. With the cards I gave them envelope with a label that read, *"on the Sunday you are ready to join, seal these eight cards in this envelope and hand them to the pastor."*

In the months that followed, 95% of the new households made the seven commitments on the Sunday they joined, including a financial pledge.

Once the church reached 400 in attendance, my associate pastor made the door step visits. Instead of me making a home visit, on the first Sunday of each month, at 7pm, I offered a "Coffee with the Pastor." On the second Sunday of every month, at 7pm I offered "Church Basics," which included a walk through the eight cards.

†††

As I said above, you don't have to buy *"Committed to Christ: Six Steps to a Generous Life."* You can design your own discipleship system.

However, after you have determined what you believe the Lord expects of deeply devoted disciples, there  are several principals I strongly suggest:

1) Include an invitation to commit to Christ.

2) Extended a holistic stewardship invitation, instead of only asking for money.

3) Place EQUAL ENERGY on each of those areas of Christian discipleship; AND

4) I also recommend that you use any social media your congregation is connected to: – twitter prayers, blogs, and facebook.

†††

There are many annual stewardship programs designed for a fall Stewardship event in a local church.

Most of them focus almost exclusively on financial gifts to the church.

As I have said repeatedly above, it seems to me that in most of our churches, the only time every household is contacted in person or by direct mail, is to ask for financial gifts. Members are often correct when they say, *"The only time the church thinks of me is when they want money."*

That, my friends, should NEVER be the case.

The call to Christian discipleship is far more broad than the typical fall stewardship campaign. *"Committed to Christ: Six Steps to a Generous Life,"* I believe, is far closer to the full range of invitations the Lord makes to each who seek to be a disciple.

†††

At the end of this forty day (six week) discipleship emphasis, members can no longer truthfully say, *"The only time the church thinks of me is when they want money."* Instead, they can truthfully say, *"My church expects a lot."*

†††

I am offering these ideas to you as a discipleship education emphasis. However, some of you are only looking for a MONEY PROGRAM.

You might be asking, *"If I am going to recommend this stewardship program to my local church, I need to know if these strategies will actually increase the per capita giving of our congregation?"*

Great question.

Research has shown that the percentage-giving strategy, if used year after year, does indeed increase the per capita giving.

Researcher Dean Hogue and his co-authors report in their book *Money Matters: Personal Giving in American Churches*, that there are three general ways that churches ask their parishioners to contribute money.

†††

The FIRST general way is called an **OFFERING CHURCH.**

- These churches do NOT hold an annual financial stewardship campaign.

- The parishioners are simply invited to respond to the offering plate each week in the pews or in a basket at the back door.

- In these churches, parishioners on average give 1.5% of their income to the church.

†††

A SECOND general way is called a **PLEDGING CHURCH.**

• In these churches, the leadership prepares an annual budget.

• Parishioners are then asked to give financial resources to support the budget.

• The message is: *"Your church needs money to accomplish the ministries described in our budget. Please give generously so that these ministries can be accomplished. Keep in mind that our budget reflects a 3% increase."*

In pledging churches, parishioners on average give 2.9% of their income to their church – about twice as much as in churches that do not ask their parishioners to pledge.

In other words, research has shown that when, year after year, a church asks parishioners to write their financial intentions on a pledge card AND turn it into the church office, on average the parishioners will give twice as much as churches who no not ask their parishioners to pledge.

Living Generously / Giving Generously: The Spiritual Discipline of Stewardship

†††

The THIRD general way that churches ask their parishioners to contribute money is called the **PERCENTAGE-GIVING CHURCH.**

• In these churches, instead of preparing an annual budget first and asking parishioners to support it, the church first conducts an annual stewardship campaign that asks parishioners: *"What percentage of your income do you feel God is calling you to give?"*

• Parishioners decide the percentage, translate it into a dollar amount, and write the dollar amount on a commitment card.

• The church then uses the total of these commitment cards, subtracting anticipated shortfall and adding anticipated loose-plate offerings, in preparing its budget.

• Herb Miller says that in percentage giving churches: parishioners are not asked to pay the bills or support the budget - rather, they are asked to grow spiritually, giving a percentage of their income to the work of the Lord through their congregation.

• In these percentage-giving churches, parishioners on average give 4.6% of their income to their church.

In other words, research has shown that when churches repeatedly ask year after year, *"What percentage of your income do you feel God is calling you to give?"* – parishioners on average give three times more dollars per year than in churches that only rely on passing the offering plate or placing a basket by the back door.

"Committed to Christ: Six Steps to a Generous Life" invites congregations to be percentage–giving churches, not focusing on the church's need to meet a budget, but rather upon each individual's need to respond generously to the saving Grace of Jesus Christ.

"Committed to Christ" is an invitation to every household in the congregation to begin and continue a life-long journey that will raise their level of commitment within each of six areas of discipleship.

†††

As you design your discipleship system, I recommend several things.

First, I recommend that it be holistic.

It's NOT just about money!

What are the steps toward Holy Living?

What are the steps toward Discipleship?

Make those steps part of the fabric of your church from day one.

Secondly, determine what commitments are indeed worthy of inviting people to give their life too.

In that process, also review the commitments that have historically framed the church's primary expectations.

Third, as you design your system, place equal emphasis on each step. Clearly communicate that this is not simply 'about money.'

Fourth, develop steps are realistic and achievable.

Living Generously / Giving Generously: The Spiritual Discipline of Stewardship

Persons who are new to the faith need to hear introductory, **first step invitations** that are engaging and challenging.

Also, the saints in your church, who have attended worship and Sunday School for their entire lives, need to hear **advanced invitations** to grow not just numerically but to grow in the the quality of their relationship to the Lord.

In the discipleship system you design, invite your congregation to a journey worthy of a lifetime.

Offer an invitation to intentionally begin, step by step, month by month, year by year a journey toward Holiness, toward Sanctification, toward winning the only race worth winning.

Invite them on a journey that is echoed in II Timothy: *"I have fought the good fight, finished the race, and kept the faith."*

†††

I wonder?

What would it be like for you and me to

personally say *"yes"* to God?

Personally – no more lukewarm, no more fence sitting, and no more spectator sport.

Personally – hot for the Gospel, fully engaged once again.

What would change at home?

What would change at work?

What would change in here in our heart?

What would it be like for you to discover a way to help your church to say *"yes"* to God?

To re-engage in the journey of making new disciples of Jesus Christ?

– a life-changing season for our churches.

– a journey worthy of giving our lives to.

†††

†††

If you are in a smaller church, perhaps a church that has never had an annual campaign nor
ever asked their members to sign a pledge card...

Here is what I am suggesting.

You don't need permission of your board or council or finance committee to do this.

The next time you preach a sermon on prayer, have blank 3x5 cards in the bulletin, in the pencil rack, or placed on every chair.

At the end of your sermon on prayer say, *"If you are ready to grow in your prayer life. If you are ready to start implementing one of the 6 ways to pray I have just mentioned in my sermon, I invite you to take the 3x5 card and simply write the word 'YES.' If you are not ready, just write 'NOT YET.' You don't have to sign the card – Jesus already knows your name. As you come to the front to receive Holy Communion (or as we sing the closing hymn) I invite you to place your card on the altar."*

If that works, and you are not 'tarred and feathered and run out of town' – a few weeks later when you preach on the importance of reading the Bible – use the same card method.

A month later, when you preach on the importance of worship attendance – use the same card method.

A month after that, when you preach on financial giving... You get the idea.

Each following month, select one of the 6 to 12 steps you have decided on.

Perhaps this becomes your pattern once a month when Holy Communion is served - each month give an invitation to make a commitment to take a specific step toward Sanctification – Holy Living – when they come forward to kneel and receive the body and blood of Christ.

Focus Point

Action Step: Now, letting all this soak in – what one or two ideas might you implement in your congregation this year?

Living Generously / Giving Generously: The Spiritual Discipline of Stewardship

Chapter Four

The basic content of this chapter was first prepared for the Stewardship Summit of the South Carolina Conference of the United Methodist Church. In preparation for that summit, I required the participants to read Clif Christopher's book, *God vs Money*. In recognition of that, I refer to that source and quote Clif Christopher about a dozen times in this presentation. Clif's book is an excellent resource, and I encourage you to purchase it at Cokesbury.com or Amazon.com.

Forty Eight Ways to Improve Your Annual Stewardship Campaign

1. If you have noticed a decline in your offering plate receipts, you are not alone. In 1968 giving to religion received close to 60% of all charitable gifts. We now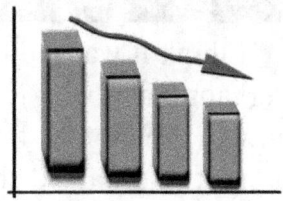

get 32%. Also, back in 2004 36% of Americans gave NOTHING to a church or other religious organization. Today, 45% give NOTHING to a church or other religious organization. (God vs Money, p. 4)

2. The enemy of stewardship is sin. It is a sin to put anything above our Lord God. Clif Christopher writes, *"a great majority of your congregation loves stuff and money more than they love God. They spend their life trying to build one more barn. They have frantic days seeking to add more to a 401(k). They desperately want to own a (second) house on the lake, thinking that if they only had one then all their weekends would have peace and joy. It consumes them. This is sin!"* (God vs Money, p. 34)

3. For some of us this Holy Habit of financial generosity may be the most difficult of *"Committed to Christ: Six Steps to a Generous Life."*

I think it was a difficult step back in Jesus' day too. Perhaps that is why Jesus talked more about 'money and how to use money' than he spoke about prayer, heaven or hell. Jesus talked about money frequently. Jesus told

43 parables recorded in the New Testament, and 27 of these parables are about money and possessions.

Jesus talked a lot about money, and I'm confident that the synagogue offering increased in every town he taught in.

4. Herb Miller has counted 500 verses in the Bible on prayer, 500 verses on faith, and more than 2,000 verses on money and what money buys.

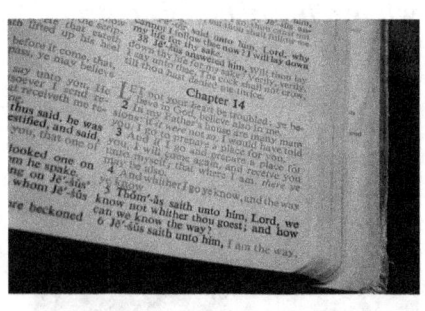

Pastors, if you are preaching from the Bible, then a reasonable rule of thumb is **at least 6 times a year our sermon should be confronting the sin of greed.** Our congregations are constantly bombarded with commercials implying that purchasing their product will lead to happiness and joy. If we are faithful to the teachings of Jesus, our sermons will be making it clear that only in Jesus Christ do we find life in all it's fullness. (God vs Money, p. 35)

5. These 48 are not offered so that you will get more money. Rather that you will use these 48 ideas to make deeply devoted disciples of Jesus Christ who are

intimately aware that God has given and blessed them

far more than anything they could ever give back to God.

Let's create disciples who do not give out of guilt or obligation, but out of *"a sincere belief that a life of generosity is a glorious life that leads to everlasting life, while a life of being controlled by stuff is a dead-end that destroys not only us but also the world around us."* (God vs Money, p. .xii)

6. Teach, preach and practice **holistic stewardship.**

Stewardship is about our relationship with God, it is NOT about paying the church bills, NOR simply something we slipped into the membership vows.

Financial giving is a part of what it means to be a deeply devoted disciple – right alongside of prayer, bible study, faithful worship attendance, hands on service, and witnessing. These are the fruits that follow a commitment to Christ.

Stewardship is about Sanctification. It is about Holy Living. It is about following Jesus.

7. Teach and preach that stewardship is a **joyful response** to God's generosity. The tithe is

not a tax, nor a clever way to pay the church's bills.

8. While the ushers are coming to the front, use that 45 seconds to share a story of a changed life in the church.

People give to change lives, not to pay the bills. For example, say something like this:

> "On Wednesday, Jennifer asked me to read a Bible story during our after school program. Little kindergartner Blake Grayson, sat right next to me. While I held the Bible in my lap, waiting for the other children to gather, Blake reached over and gently touched the Bible. He whispered to me – 'Preacher, I love the Bible.'
>
> His simple words touched me, and it took me a moment to gain my composure before I could read to the children.
>
> Thank you! Thank you for supporting this church with your generous gifts. Your gifts are making a difference right here with our children – and in missions we support in a 100 countries around this world. Thank you."

Tell stories of how lives have been changed because of their giving. People need to know their giving makes a difference.

Living Generously / Giving Generously: The Spiritual Discipline of Stewardship

9. The offering should be **high and holy moment** within every worship service. It is not a necessary evil. It is not fund raising. It is an act of worship, responding to free gift of God's grace.

Clif Christopher writes, *"Every week as you plan the sermon, hymns and anthems, pay attention that the offering does not come across as an afterthought. How can you be certain that it is lifted up to feel a full and important part of our living out our calling to be a generous disciple?"* (God vs Money, p. 81)

10. **Set a good example** – the offering plate should be seen passing through the band, choir, instrumentalist, and pastors on stage. The congregation needs to see the pastor placing a gift in the offering plate in every worship service.

11. Clif Christopher states that pastors and leaders in the church must model the life they preach about, especially

– 100 –

in the area where our people struggle the most - their dependence on stuff. *"As pastors we have to model how we manage, spend, and give our money. Money is the chief enemy of the disciple-to-be... Pastors are not immune to temptation, but through Christ they have learned a better way. It is this better way of living and giving that must be seen by (the congregation)... For pastors this means we model the life of a generous disciple at Walmart, at a restaurant, at deer camp, or the movie theater. Wherever we are, we are called to set an example of what it means to have surrendered control to Jesus."* (God vs Money, p. 11)

12. Clif Christopher writes, *"Today is the best day to decide that you have to get your life right before you can help others to get theirs right.*  *You have to find a way to have your house in order before you discuss the need for them to get their houses in order. Today is the best day to decide to get debt's dominance out of your life. You may need a good financial or credit counselor, or you may be able to make a plan yourself. But do it today.*

Today is the best day to decide to begin giving in a way that reflects gratitude and grace. Today is the best day to determine that the one debt you have to fix is the debt to God. Maybe you have to sell something. Maybe

Living Generously / Giving Generously: The Spiritual Discipline of Stewardship

you have to downsize your vehicle. Maybe you have to decide not to take any vacations away from home. Maybe you change the way you shop for clothes or how often you eat out. Maybe you change your giving habits on birthdays, anniversaries, and holidays. But one way or another, make your giving to God a priority." (God vs Money, p. 17)

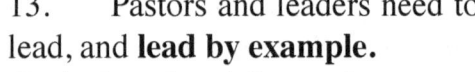

13. Pastors and leaders need to lead, and **lead by example.**

In the last church I served as pastor, in preparation for **the Church Nominations process:**

I had my assistant take the membership list and put a check mark by each individual with "outstanding attendance."

Then the small group coordinator put a check mark by each member who was active in a "small group."

Finally the treasurer put a check mark by each member who was a "generous financial giver" based on Jesus' math.

The names with 3 check marks formed the pool of names for the nomination's committees work. (similar theme in God vs Money, p. 45)

14. As you are considering adding part time **staff**, inviting members of the congregation to fill those positions, be sure

the one you hire also has "**three check marks by their name.**"

15. Choose a **time of year** when there is a high probability of connecting with the most people. Often this is October/ November. It could also be mid-January/February.

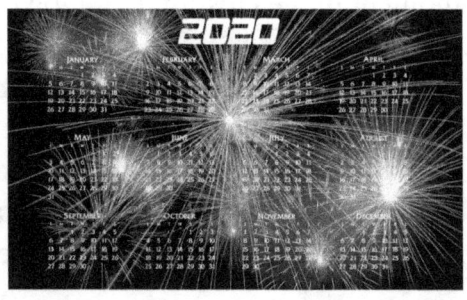

16. Set a **realistic time line**. In a large church, planning and implementation can take six months or more.

17. **Avoid the temptation to rush** this through.

If you are asking your current givers to consider increasing their gift – they need time for those discussions at home.

If you are asking people to consider giving for the first time in their lives – they need time for those discussions at home.

Preachers, I know your sermons are the best in the

country – however your congregation will not make this important of a decision, and stick to it, on the spur of the moment in the closing invitation of your sermon.

18. **Avoid the temptation to have your annual program stand alone.** It should be part of a year-round approach to discipleship education.

19. Be **realistic about your expectations** from the annual program. Increases in giving are typically incremental – not astronomical.

One of the great things about Herb Miller's *"Consecration Sunday"* is that he asks for incremental growth over time. He suggests, if you are currently NOT giving, consider a gift of $5 a week. If you are currently giving $5 a Sunday, step up to $10, or from $20 to $30, or from $100 to $125.

"Committed to Christ: Six Steps to a Generous Life" also follows this invitation model of *"climb one step"*.

Living Generously / Giving Generously: The Spiritual Discipline of Stewardship

20. The goal is NOT equal gifts. NEVER divide the budget by the number of households and say, *"If every household would give $5,000..."* Your households do not have equal resources. Also, such comments are counter productive – it does not inspire the non-giver  to start giving because they perceive you've just asked them to make an astronomical gift, and it may give permission for your most generous givers **to cut back** on their giving because you have just asked them to reduce their gift to $5,000!

Remember that in Jesus' math, the goal is **equal sacrifice**. The widow's $30 may represent a 10% tithe of her resources that week. The teenagers' $3 gift may be more than a tithe. The professional couples' $30 gift may represent less than 1% of their resources that week.

21. Do not ask people to give to the budget. No one cares about a budget. People care about children, youth, the sick, the environment, the lost, broken hearts and broken lives.

Write out a brief and compelling case as to how *"contributing to your church will change lives and make the world the place God intended it to be."* (God vs Money, p. 60)

If your case statement isn't compelling to you, then go back and work on it until it is compelling. Scattered throughout the year, this **brief and compelling paragraph** should be a part of sermons, and the pastor's weekly blog.

22. **Put together a team to lead** each annual campaign. For any stewardship campaign to succeed, it must truly be a congregational effort, with many people involved at several different levels.

Bad Idea: Is for the entire program is "run" by the pastor and office assistant, with a lay figurehead willing to have letters sent over their signature.

Good Idea: The program invites 10% to 20% of the active congregation to play some level of leadership. Instead of looking for ways to simplify and fast-track the campaign, the stewardship campaign will be far more effective and fruitful if ways are explored to involve more people in the process.

23. The **team leader should be a faithful giver**, preferably someone who tithes at least 10% of their income.

24. The **team should include every age level**, and the different active ministry areas of your church all designed to help build a sense of ownership in the outcome.

25. The **team should include the generous givers** of your church, as well as the poor widow.

26. Ask the **team members to make their pledges first.** As leaders, ask them to lead in this way as a sign of their commitment and to encourage the balance of the congregation to also make a pledge.

27. Ask the **team to be a part of your comprehensive communication** strategy. Use every available method:

sermons, music, testimony in worship, bulletin, newsletter, web site, twitter, facebook, blogs, bulletin boards, banners, and their testimony in each small group they are a part of.

28. Remember to **actually ASK people to give**, across all your communication mediums, including the sermon. Many people never give because they have never been asked.

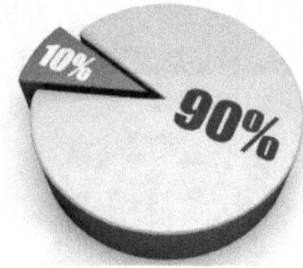

29. Remember **the 90 / 10 rule**. In almost every church 90% of the funds come from 10% of the congregation. Most of your **new** funds this year will also come from your current generous givers. The 10% need your personal attention and relationship. **Also, don't neglect the 90%** – they need invitations to **begin to grow** toward the tithe, but it will be a 6 to 8 year process.

30. Pastors - you have a unique relationship with people who have had a

recent death in their household.

You have a unique relationship with people who are thinking about getting married this June

You have a unique relationship with the people in the *Disciple Bible* class you taught.

You have a unique relationship with people who are facing a personal crises.

You have a unique relationship with the adults you have baptized this year.

Pastors - you should also have a **unique relationship with the 10 to 20 households who are the major financial contributors** to your congregation, and those with the potential of making a major gift. Two or three times a year this group of major donors should be among the first to be asked for their hopes and dreams for the church, and also be the first to hear your personal hopes and dreams for the church. (similar theme in God vs Money, p 58-59)

31. Pastors, a significant percentage of your offering comes from five to ten families. These families must be visited on a one-to-one basis by the pastor. During that visit  the pastor should ask the family to give to the church in the coming year. Obviously the ask depends some on what is going on in the church but generically:

"Joe and Mary, before I move forward to the congregation for their commitments I need to show

Living Generously / Giving Generously: The Spiritual Discipline of Stewardship

support and leadership from a handful. Would the two of you consider growing your commitment for 2020 to $20,000?"

OR

"Jack and Susan, the two of you have led the way in financial stewardship for some time. We could not succeed without you. Would you be willing to consider a gift of $20,000 for our 2020 campaign and lead us again?"

The key parts are: personal, short, direct, and "consider" a specific number you suggest.

This of course is followed by grace and thanks. *(Clif Christopher)*

32. Pastors, during the summer, plan on going to lunch once a week solely to learn about how and why they give to the church. Include the widow who gives two coins, as well as those who give a significant portion of your offering. *"This lunch is a fishing expedition. You want to know why they give. How do they determine what is right to give? What is their story in coming to the church and coming to faith in Christ? What do they have a real passion for? If they could do anything in the church right now to make it better, what would it be? You are putting numerous hooks in the water asking one probing question after another*

as you learn about this person" (God vs Money, p. 88) and whether he or she might be open to increasing their giving.

In making these appointments, I met with Janet. It turns out, in Jesus' math, Janet was the largest contributor to my church. Janet never married. She was physically disabled. She would not accept federal assistance of any kind, instead she worked part-time at the school cafeteria as her health allowed. She lived in a one room apartment, and gave $6 every Sunday. To give that much so she had to adjust her grocery shopping, and eat more macaroni and less tuna fish. When we had a building campaign, she doubled her giving to $12.

At the time my wife and I were giving $245 every Sunday. We had discovered the joy of giving 20% – double tithing. However, unlike Janet, our level of giving never affected our grocery shopping. I am **not** as generous as Janet, and in Jesus' math, Janet gives far more money to the church than I do.

33. Make giving by **automatic withdrawal from checking accounts** simple for persons to choose when making their pledges.

Understand the financial patterns in your community. If very few people carry cash, an impulse offering will not work.

Remember that typically older women are more

likely to carry a checkbook than older men. Younger generations do not carry checkbooks, or even have one, since they are more inclined to pay electronically. A 25 year old is not likely to make a gift of stock, while an older member might be interested in an estate gift.

34. In addition to automatic drafts from checking accounts, consider the use of online giving, QR code giving, kiosk giving, and any other form of e-giving you can. Richard Roger's book, *"The E-Giving Guide for Every Church"* is an excellent resource. His book will remove the confusion and fear about electronic giving and open your church to new possibilities.

35. **Be positive in everything** you communicate. People respond to positive language. Few people will give generously to a church in financial distress that communicates that it is about to close.

FOLLOW THROUGH

36. Send a **personalized thank you letter** immediately after the program. Do not send a "Dear member" form letter. Send a personal typed or better yet, a hand written note, signed by the pastor.

37. Throughout the year, in churches with 350+ in attendance, each week 5 to 10 thank you notes should be written to donors who have given financially or given of their time to the work of the church that week. (God vs Money, p. 80)

38. Throughout the year, when the church receives an unusually large financial gift, send a **personalized thank you letter** immediately.

39. Throughout the year, **find multiple occasions to say "thank you"** and report on changed lives because of their giving - in the sermons, newsletters, blogs, website and bulletins.

40. **Prepare the budget AFTER your stewardship program.** The Lord has just revealed your anticipated income, so set the budget accordingly. Use the total of the commitment cards, subtract anticipated shortfall, add active donors who may not have turned in a card, and add anticipated loose-plate offerings in preparing the budget.

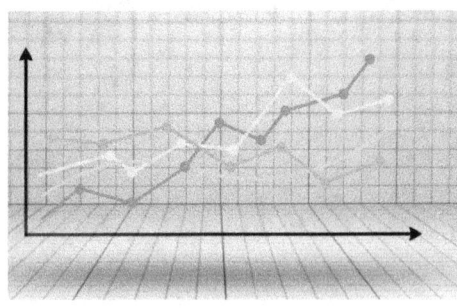

41. The best indicator of future giving is past giving. Look at a ten year record of total receipts, and keep that trend in mind

when projecting next years offering. If your largest giver has died or moved recently, keep that in mind as well in preparing the budget.

42. Once the detailed budget is prepared, make it available to all who ask, but **do NOT mail it to everyone.** Instead, **prepare a Missional Budget**, that in narrative form indicates that, for example, $80,000 provides meaningful, life changing worship each week; $37,000 nurtures persons in their faith journey; and $83,000 to witness to our faith in service beyond ourselves; totaling $200,000 to fulfill our mission of *"Changing Lives for Christ."*

43. Clif Christopher suggest that large churches of 350+ in attendance should send out monthly giving statements, and that smaller churches should send statements every quarter.

44. Be sure the giving **statement, looks more like a thank you letter** than a bill from VISA. The letter should include a ministry story, letting them know what the church has done to change lives this year.

45. If your church does not send quarterly statements, be sure and **at least send one** the Monday after Thanksgiving. This will give families several weeks to catch up their giving if they have fallen behind. (God vs Money, p.79)

46. Quarterly, publish a **detailed wish list** of items that would help your ministry be more effective. Some of these items may already be included in your operating budget. The list might include new chairs for the choir, a new van for the senior citizens, new cribs for the nursery, or a new piano for the sanctuary.

Be sure and list the exact model number, color, size, and exact cost for each item. Your music department doesn't want my grandmothers old piano, they want a *"Baldwin Ebony Baby Grand Piano model M, costing $5,132 including tax and delivery."*

Your nursery department doesn't want my old hand-me-down crib either. They want a *'Graco model #8965 for $339.86 including mattress, tax, and delivery."*

I made a mistake one time on a major gift of a replacement steeple. I forgot to include tax and installation!

47. Every January, with the new year, offer a personal finance class at the church using Dave Ramsay's "Financial Peace University" OR Crown Financial Ministries: MANAGING OUR FINANCES GOD'S WAY."

48. Lay leadership - part of our job as church leaders is to identify and enlist church persons who not only have the capacity to give significant gifts, but also more importantly the **will** to do so. This coming year, *"just by spending a little bit of time, using some common sense,*

and buying a couple of lunches you can discover things far more valuable than" what a demographic report will tell you. (God vs Money p. 85)

BONUS IDEAS

In addition to your annual campaign we've been talking about, there are two bonus ideas.

Bonus idea #1.
Many in our congregations have accumulated assets like stocks, bonds, property, insurance, and inherited funds. Every college, hospital, and most major non-profit organizations are asking your members to make gifts from these assets every day.

If someone in your congregation inherits a great deal of money from their aged parents, and they want to donate a considerable amount in their memory – they will immediately consider the local hospital, college, Red Cross or American Cancer Society. Why? Because

Living Generously / Giving Generously: The Spiritual Discipline of Stewardship

they have been asked to.

In your church, have your trustees and council develop and make available an list of ministry dreams. Make sure that you have a **clear and concise plan, and options, for a gift of $10,000, $50,000, $100,000 or $1 million dollars** if someone walked in tomorrow with a check and asked you what could be done with it. (see also, God vs Money, p. 48-49)

Bonus idea #2.

Every person in your congregation will eventually die. When they die, in many cases there will be an estate left behind of property, homes, stocks, bonds, and life insurance. Many of your members have already remembered to include the local hospital, college, Red Cross or American Cancer Society in their will. Why? Because they have been asked to.

Every church should be inviting members to remember the church in their will. Invite them to add the phrase: *"I wish 10% of my estate to go to Union United Methodist Church in Irmo, South Carolina."*

On page 50-52 of *"God vs Money"*, Clif Christopher outlines a simple way to get Bonus idea #2 organized and started in your church. (God vs Money, p. 50-52)

†††

Conclusion

Over all, we are offering a loud and consistent biblical message that Jesus Christ calls us to live generously. We understand what is truly valuable in life.

It is not what kind of house you have, not what kind of car you drive, not the clothes you wear, not how much money you have...

It has a whole lot more to do with words like faith, family, friends...

It has more to do with, *"What kind of heart do you have?"* and *"How has your life-style of generosity changed lives?"*

Focus Point

Action Step: What are additional ways we could improve our annual stewardship campaigns?

Action Step: What one or two might you implement this year in your local church?

Stewardship Resources from Horizons Stewardship

I have hired and relied on the great team at Horizon's for decades. They are amazing people who love the Lord and are ready and able to come by your side and enrich your stewardship ministry. A few of their resources are below:

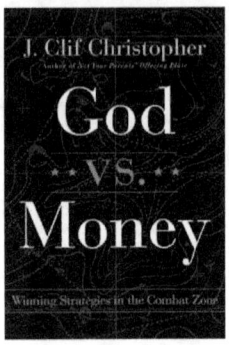

www.horizons.net

www.ingramcontent.com/pod-product-compliance
Lightning Source LLC
Chambersburg PA
CBHW070432010526
44118CB00014B/2018